TURNING SQUARE CORNERS WITH THE GOVERNMENT[1]

INTRODUCTION

Administrative Agencies are tasked with making policy via various instruments. These instruments are relied on by government employees, third parties, and every day citizens like you and me. Every day experience with our government doe not deviate far from every day experience of the average Joe Schmoe.

For example, as a child of social security myself, every part of my childhood life rest on the benefits provided by the welfare system every month. That is, until my mother graduated Nursing school where she was able

---

[1] "Men must turn square corners when they deal with the Government" Rock Island, A.& L.R. Co. v. United States, 254 U.S. 141, 143 (1920) (Holmes, J.)

to receive a modified version of the welfare assistance based on the level of care should could provide henceforth.

This welfare provided for the quality of life that I experienced from a very young age and all the way through my educational experience. Although the quality of life can not be compared to others in more comfortable positions, the welfare was able to provide for a bed to rest in, a roof over my head, and an education.

And, I was able to choose my own path. Where my oldest brother just finished his service with the Air-Force, where I have been in school my whole life: private education, pre-school, public school, private college, and private law school.

Additionally, I volunteered when I had time to give back to my community: YMCA, churches, air force and army reserves, LAPD, natural disaster(s), afterschool autism, federal income tax, and finally at the SBA's

NDLRC. All of these events, I was there along with everyone else turning left corners with the Government / turning pages with the government.

Now, with my education, I wish to share my experience where I have been tasked by the SBA's NDRLC in creating a quick reference guide for loan officers. Therefore, I invite you to turn square corners with the Government and I, as I describe a specific issue the SBA'S NDRLC has had and a detailed explanation on how to fix that issue and many others to come.

I.   THE TASK

Recently, I had the opportunity to work with the Small Business Association's National Disaster Resolution Solution Center –through a voluntary internship- on an *Amicus Curiae* brief.[2] There, I was assigned the following

---

[2] *Amicus Curiae* brief disclosed upon approval of Chief Counsel

issue: Whether SBA because the proper hearing officer's decision by its own terms applied only to loan 2860140-09 and not to 27860145-10?[3].

There, an SBA employee made a mistake and recorded the initial loan as cleared and changed the loan as well as its status and obligation to paid in full.[4]At first glance, this issue does not itself seem too important. But, a closer look shows that this particular loan carried a balance of $1,000,000.00. That is, the employee's mistake could have potentially cost the Government a chunk of change.[5]

My first step in discovering a solution, following that experience, I wrote a memorandum after researching the modern extension of Collateral Estoppel to Administrative agency decisions over -whether an alternative rule could be adopted by the court in particularized cases to protect

---

pending as of *May 15th 2016*.
[3] See Id. at pending approval *see infra* at FN 8.
[4] See Id. at pending approval *see infra* at FN 8
[5] See Id. at pending approval *see infra* at FN 8

the natural inefficiency and unfairness of these decisions when using Collateral Estoppel.[6]

There, I discovered because of the lack of neutrality between these functions and a heavy reliance on policy and particularized disputes, Administrative agency decisions are naturally susceptible to the inefficiency and unfairness of the effects of Collateral Estoppel.[7] This consequence also severally undermines and threatens the adjudicative advantages shared by Administrative Agencies.[8]

Then, I was given a task to create the quick reference guide we have discussed for loan officers for the SBA.[9]

1) Currently, loan officers and specialist at the SBA, specifically the NDLRC use an outdated reference guide[10]

2) Here are some of the identified problems with the

---

[6] *See* attached document: Memorandum.
[7] *See* Id.
[8] *See* Id.
[9] *See* attached correspondence: pending approval *see infra* at FN 8.
[10] *See* attached correspondence: pending approval *see infra* at FN 8.

current system: very comprehensive, very long, officers

and specialist find it intimidating, and could focus on

particular issues and not so much on others[11]

3) Based off notes from the Chief Counsel and the

Foreclosure Counsel, off a primer from an SBA attorney,

loan specialist and officers suggestions and comments, and

an old reference guide from the SBA; here is how we fix

the current reference guide and how the new reference

guide is better and important:[12]

a) The reference guide will be a 1-page summary making

each action, accrue, and authority more accessible and

reader friendly (in plain english);[13]

b) Specifically, the reference guide consists of several

dimensions for the visual presentation (the layout of the

information or data): there are several visual forms for this

---

[11] *See* attached correspondence: pending approval *see infra* at FN 8.
[12] *See* attached correspondence: pending approval *see infra* at FN 8.
[13] *See* attached correspondence: pending approval *see infra* at FN 8.

information, therefore the reference guide will display information in several formats- where the loan officers and specialist can use the chart as a visual reference (and) interact with the chart analytically[14]

c) The guide will be able to assist the loan officers and specialists on specific issues and several sub-issues, as accurately as possible: through a visual analysis- the loan officer or specialist may follow each step and come to a conclusion (one that may be 'double-checked' using the chart);[15]

d) And additionally,

i) for the NDLRC's purposes, procurement contract, duplication of benefits, and re-commence dismissed claims shall be deleted as necessary; and[16]

ii) for Administrative wage garnishment purposes, insert

---

[14] *See* attached correspondence: pending approval *see infra* at FN 8.
[15] *See* attached correspondence: pending approval *see infra* at FN 8.
[16] *See* attached correspondence: pending approval *see infra* at FN 8.

may be subject to defense of latches; and[17]

iii) for Foreclosure purposes, focus on Florida, Texas, Louisiana, North Carolina, Mississippi for SOL's on mortgages and deeds, as well as, judicial and non-judical foreclosures (on SOL on federal tax return offset, administrative wage garnishment, trigger date, and the filing of bankruptcy's effect on SOLs. [18]

I was tasked with creating a document that may very well put an employee in the very same position as described above.[19] Therefore, I was determined to discover a way of eliminating this inconsistency, this liability. I was determined to find progress in turning square corners with the government.[20]

II. THE TOOLS

---

[17] *See* attached correspondence: pending approval *see infra* at FN 8.
[18] *See* attached correspondence: pending approval *see infra* at FN 8.
[19] *See* Id. *infra* at FN 8.
[20] *See* Id. at *infra* FN 1.

Now that the task's purpose has been outline, let us take a look at the legal basis behind the creation of such document(s) or instruments and the following policy consequences.

An agency, like any individual or entity, may choose to apply its authority, that is policy decisions, through guidance documents, interpretative rules, policy statements, handbooks, manuals, directives, and Memorandum of Understanding.[21]

And other tools, such as: internal guidelines, staff material, forms used within agencies, and third parties with those who they deal.[22] Each application having its own reasoning and nature, and therefore the agency will be held responsible for the authority promulgated through these means for those reasons.[23]

---

[21] Cass; Diver; Beermann; and Freeman, "Administrative Law: Case and Materials- Chapter IV. 'Choice of Policymaking Instruments'", (7h edition Wolters Kluwer Law & Business 416-427 NY 2016).
[22] See Id. at 416

a. Less visible means of policy making

The purpose(s) for a less visible means of policy making could be a response to the difficulties inherent in making decisions via rulemaking and formal adjudication, that is, costly, time consuming, and difficult to reverse as circumstances change[24].

Perhaps, a less visible means of policy making, like a quick reference guide, can be produced relatively quickly.[25] The quick reference guide can also be easily changed as opposed to a comprehensive rule, that is, infusing flexibility into the policy making process.[26] In larger agencies, where responsibility is diffused and subject to numerous interpretation, the decision is likely inconsistent.[27] Therefore, less visible policy is inherent in

---

[23] *See* Id. at 417
[24] *See* id. at 424
[25] *See* id.
[26] *See* id.
[27] *See* id.

larger agencies.[28]

In conclusion, a spectrum of policymaking exists for Agencies via instruments with respect to the authority extended by Congress and the decisions to promulgate that authority.

b. Least formal method of agency policy making

The least formal method of agency policy making, a step further towards rulemaking is "jawboning".[29] This is where Regulators use their influence over regulated parties to nudge their behavior in a certain discretion without taking any step toward formal policymaking.[30]

Policy is arrived at informally and implemented informally, that is, where Regulators urge a regulated party to voluntarily adopt a code of good conduct in line with the Regulators view.[31]

---

[28] *See* id.
[29] *See* id. at 424
[30] *See* id.
[31] *See* id.

This strategy depends on an implicit threat[32]. The threat may lie in a regulated party's need for continuing agency cooperation[33]. An example where the Federal Communications Commission used its authority as a licensing agency to influence television licensees to agree to a family friendly hour of prime time programming.[34]

In conclusion, Agencies can use Environmental disasters and other circumstances as a bargaining chip to promulgate policy in a less formal means.

c. Legal Basis for Agency decision

And what follows, is the legal basis for that decisions.[35] In *Ruiz,* there involved no such formal procedures: there was no outside participation in drafting the manual.[36] *Ruiz* does not hold the BIA policy

---

[32] *See* id.
[33] *See* id.
[34] *See* Id.; (*See* the Writers Guild case, excreted at p. 821, *infra)*
[35] See Id. at 422.

substantively invalid, but instead indicates that the

Secretary and the Bureau failed to use a policymaking

process appropriate to create such a rule.[37]

In Bel, there involved a change of policy arrived at-

or at least announced- with the aid of formal procedures,

albeit not rulemaking.[38] A distinction could lead to

agencies never making policy by informal means.[39]

In conclusion, every actions taken by the Agencies is a

step towards the legal basis for that decision.

d. Fairness

If there were a line to draw on the spectrum of an

Agencies policymaking, that line is drawn between these

other policy formations and plain rulemaking with the

fairness stick.[40] For example, in *Bell* and *Ruiz* the court

---

[36] *See* id.
[37] *See* id.
[38] *See* id.
[39] *See* id.
[40] *See* id. at 422

will approve policy formulation other than by rulemaking, but only so long as new policy is not applied to any "unsuspecting" party.[41]

In conclusion, where this concept does not completely limit an Agencies policymaking discretion- it colors it.

e. The Cast

But, once the line is drawn, the policy formations and plain rulemaking can be as if they were set in stone with § 552(a)(2)(c).[42] The APA requires that administrative staff manuals and other instructions to administrators that affect members of the public be published and that an agency may not rely on unpublished material to affect adversely members of the public.[43]

In Smith v. National Transp. Safety Bd., 981 F.2d (D.C. Cir. 1993),[44] the Court relied on above provision to

---

[41] *See* id.
[42] *See* id. AT 422-23.
[43] *See* Id. at 423
[44] Smith v. National Transp. Safety Bd., 981 F.2d (D.C. Cir. 1993).

invalidate the suspension of a commercial pilot's license[45]. The court's reasoning rested on the idea that a cast of the policy was set because the agency relied on an unpublished FFA bulletin[46].

In conclusion, although the fairness concept does not limit Agencies discretion in policy making, taking an action, especially a fair one, can limit the Agencies to decisions made in the past.

f. Policy making via guidance documents, interpretative rules and policy statements

Given the casting effect of certain types of policy formations and plain rulemaking -when making policy via guidance documents, interpretative rules, and policy statements- agencies are able to escape the procedural requirements governing rulemaking in certain cases and in

---

[45] *See* Id.
[46] *See* Id.

other cases are cast down as too broad.[47]

Agencies rely heavily on informal guidance documents, interpretative rules, or general policy statements to elaborate agency policy.[48] Where it is usually limited to notice and comment rulemaking[49] and widely used and voluminous[50]. APA §553(b)(3)(A) exempts "interpretative rules" and "general statements of policy" from the procedural requirements governing rulemaking, and does not mention guidance documents at all.[51]

In Apppalachian Power Co. v. EPA, 208 F.3d 1015 (D.C. Cir. 2000),[52] D.C. Circuit held that the guidance document "significantly broadened" the underlying

---

[47] *See* Id.
[48] *See* Id. at 423-424
[49] *See* Id. (See Nina A. Mendelson, Guidance Documents and Regulatory Beneficiaries, Admin. & Reg. L. News, Summer 2006, at 8 (noting that EPA and OSHA issued over 2,000 and 1,600 guidance documents respectively in a three-year period and that these documents "range from routine matters to broad policies on program standards, implementation and enforcement")
[50] *See* Id.
[51] Apppalachian Power Co. v. EPA, 208 F.3d 1015 (D.C. Cir. 2000).
[52] *See* Id.

regulations and thus was invalid because it was promulgated without notice and comment.[53]

"The phenomenon we see .. Congress passes a broadly worded statue. The agency follows with regulations containing broad language, open-ended phrases, ambiguous standards ….as years pass, the agency issues circulars or guidance or memoranda, explaining, interpreting, defining and often expanding the commands in the regulation….

One guidance document may yield another and then another and so on. Several words in a regulation may spawn hundreds of pages of text as the agency offers more and more detail regarding what its regulations demand of regulated entities".[54] In conclusion, because Agency work

---

[53] See Id.

yields even more work, an Agency spawns, that is, produces policymaking and rulemaking by continuously casting detail in words.

III.   THE BOOKS, MANUALS, AND DIRECTIVES

A step further towards rulemaking, involves the Agencies use of handbooks, manuals, and directives.[55] The Forest Service tends to develop complex and thorough internal documentation in the form of handbooks, manuals, and directives.[56] So, we shall start here.

Issues directives to its employees with respect to which are codified in manuals or handbooks.[57] The manuals offer guidance of a general application.[58] The Handbook are

---

[54] *See* Id. at 423

55 Charles A. Breer & Scot W. Anderson, "Regulation Without Rulemaking: The Force and Authority of Informal Agency Action", Davis Graham & Stubbs LLP (originally published by the Rocky Mountain Mineral Law Foundation).

[56] *See* Id.

[57] *See* Id.

[58] *See* Id.

more specialized and technical.[59] The Directives can be

supplemented by Regional Foresters and Forest

Supervisors.[60]

The Directives in handbook and manual are intended to

be binding, or[61] provide direction only to Forest Service

employees (not the public)[62]. If an employee acts because

of statement in handbook or manual there may be

consequences. [63]

    a. Handbooks, Manuals, and Directives[64]

MSHA, for example: handbook, and Program

Information Bulletins and Procedure Instruction Letters.[65]

---

[59] *See* Id.
[60] *See* Id.
[61] *See* Id.
[62] *See* Id.
[63] *See* Id.
[64] Charles A. Breer & Scot W. Anderson, "Regulation Without Rulemaking: The Force and Authority of Informal Agency Action", Davis Graham & Stubbs LLP (originally published by the Rocky Mountain Mineral Law Foundation).

- "Men must turn square corners when they deal with the Government" Rock Island, A.& L.R. Co. v. United States, 254 U.S. 141, 143 (1920) (Holmes, J.)

[65] *See* Id.

Also detailed guidance to mine inspectors for Coal Mine Health Inspection Procedures handbook ("BLM") directive system similar to Forest Services.[66]

Aside from handbook and manual- state agencies offer instructions to employees which is available online.[67]These manuals and handbooks carry a lot of weight with agencies.[68] In Rio de Viento, Inc., Interior Board of Land Appeals ask to determine what costs should properly be considered in determining whether a well was producing in paying quantities.[69] Section of BLM was at dispute, and the draft had been implemented through an Instruction Memorandum ("IM").[70] Therefore, although expired several years before, it was brought back to life.[71]

b. Memorandum of Understanding

---

[66] *See* Id.
[67] *See* Id.
[68] *See* Id.
[69] Rio de Viento, Inc.
[70] *See* Id.
[71] *See* Id.

Administrative agencies will often enter into Memoranda of Understanding (MOUs) to sort out ambiguities relating to their respective programs. These MOUs will parse out enforcement authority, jurisdiction, and territory.[72] Thus, an internal MOU can have considerable effect on the regulated community, where the MOU can change he permitting process, enforcement oversight, or where to go for guidance.[73]

An MOU in Indian Country, where there is a questions of jurisdiction, can be uncertain.[74] If a person has a permit from the tribe for an activity, and then an MOU suddenly requires a permit from a state or federal agency, the regulated party can accrue considerable risk even after having sought to comply with the regulations applicable to its activities.[75]

---

[72] *See* Id.
[73] *See* Id.
[74] *See* Id.

In, <u>Union Oil Company v. Farmington Indian Minerals Office.</u>, an Appeal decision reached by Farmington Indian Minerals Office.[76] The Office was created through a MOU between Bureau of Indian Affairs, the bureau of land management, and Minerals Management Services.[77] Because the court could not figure out which office was rending decision, it was dismiss for lack of jurisdiction.[78]

    c. Agencies Discretion to Make Policy by manual or informal guidance

Specifically, Agencies usually apply their discretion in making policy by manual or informal guidance, such as a quick reference guide.[79] Below, we shall go through a manual developed over years authorized by Congress.

---

[75] *See* Id.
[76] <u>Union Oil Company v. Farmington Indian Minerals Office.</u>
[77] *See* Id.
[78] *See* Id.
[79] *See* Id.

Congress has expressly authorized Secretary of Department of Homeland Security ("DHS")[80]: to establish national immigration enforcement policies and priorities 6 U.S.C § 202(5)[81]; to establish such regulations; … issue instructions; and perform such other acts as he deems necessary for carrying out his authority 8 U.S.C. § 1103(a)(3)[82].

Years authority can forbear certain removals[83]. Nov. 2014, issued MOU extending that policy of forbearance (see DAPA memo in pdf).[84] DAPA Memo: DHS's policy with respect to agency's exercise of its statutory enforcement discretion.[85]

Rather than substantive legal rights or imposing substantive legal obligations[86], they Advises public of

---

[80] *See* Id.
[81] *See* Id.
[82] *See* Id.
[83] *See* Id.
[84] *See* Id.
[85] *See* Id.

manner agency proposes to exercise a discretionary power. [87] As such, the DAPA Memo falls within the Administrative[88] Procedure Act's ("APA") definition of a "general statement of policy," which is exempt from notice and comment requirements.[89]

5 U.S.C § 553(b)(A)[90] allows agencies to issue "interpretative rules, general statements of policy, or rules of agency organization, procedure, or practice" without engaging in notice and comment.[91] The 5h circuit adopted an erroneous legal standard -> DAPA memo was not a general statement of policy.[92] Because did not "genuinely

---

[86] *See* Id.
[87] Lincoln v. Vigil, 508 U.S. 182, 197 (1993)
- (quoting Attorney General's Manual on the Administrative Procedure Act 30 n.3 (1947) ("AG Manual"))).

[88] *See* Id.
[89]*See* Id. (quoting Chrysler Corp. v. Brown, 441 U.S. 281, 302 n.31 (1979)
[90] *See* Id.
[91] *See* Id.
[92] *See* Id.

leave the agency and its employees free to exercise discretion".[93]

An agency pronouncement binds lower-level agency officials does not mean it is a legislative rule rather than a policy statement for APA purposes.[94] This ensures policies are reliably carried out[95] and w/o would fundamentally impair agency heads'.[96]Erred where stating policy statement's "substantial impact" on third parties is that it requires comment and notice.[97]

Comment and notice required to have legal binding effect on members of public,[98]no textual support for substantial impact.[99] The fact that individuals who qualify for deferred action under DAPA memo may then request

---

[93] Texas v. Uunited States., 809 F.3d 134, 176 (5th Cir. 2015)
[94] *See* Id.
[95] *See* Id.
[96] *See* Id.
[97] creating rights and obligations, and not practical effects (*See* 3 Pierce § 17.3, at 1572; (*See* Texas)
[98] *See* Id.
[99] *See* Id.

work authorization does not transform memo into a substantive rule.[100] The work authorization requirement is the rule adopted through notice and comment.[101] Courts do not impose additional procedural requirements on agencies beyond those mandated by the APA.[102] In order for an Agency to avoid further procedural requirement, advice would be to not ignore court's precedence [103] and do not expand notice and comment requirement.[104]

IV.   Agency Discretion to Make Policy by Manual or Informal Guidance

---

[100] *See* Id.
[101] See Final Rule, Control of Employment of Aliens, 52 Fed. Reg. 16,216 (May 1, 1987
[102] *See* Id.; (Perez v. Mortgage Bankers Association, 135 S. Ct. 1199 (2015)
[103] *See* Id.
[104] *See* Id.

In <u>Morton v. Ruiz</u>, 415 U.S. 199 (1974)[105] Blackum

wrote the opinion over an agency tasked with the

administration of the federal general assistance program

for needy Indians.[106] There, Blackum was tasked with

deciding whether the welfare assistance was available on

and ok the reservation location.[107]

In 1940, Ramon Ruize and his wife, Anita (who are

Papago Indians and United States citizens) left Papago

Reservation in Arizona to seek employment 15 miles away

at the Phelps-Dodge copper mines at Ajo.[108]They settled in

a community called the "Indian Village" which was

populated by mostly Papago Indians.[109] Phelps-Dodge

owned most of the property in the area[110] and they had

---

[105] <u>Morton v. Ruiz</u>, 415 U.S. 199 (1974).
[106] *See* Id.
[107] *See* Id.
[108] *See* Id.
[109] *See* Id.
[110] *See* Id.

lived there 7 years continuously.[111] A minor daughter lives with them[112] and they speak Papago but limited English.[113]

Have not been assimilated into the dominant culture (aside from work) (and) appear to maintain a close to with nearby reservation.[114] 27 years later, miner was shut down by strike.[115] They sought welfare assistance,[116] and the state's policy that striking workers are not[117] eligible for general assistance or emergency relief. [118]

Then, applied for general assistance via Bureau of Indian Affairs (BIA)[119] and immediately notified by letter that he was ineligible[120]. Because of the provision (in effect since 1952) in 66 Indian Affairs Manual 3.1.4

---

[111] *See* Id.
[112] *See* Id.
[113] *See* Id.
[114] *See* Id.
[115] *See* Id.
[116] *See* Id.
[117] *See* Id.
[118] *See* Id.
[119] *See* Id.
[120] *See* Id.

(1965)[121]- that eligibility is limited to Indians living "on reservations" and in jurisdictions under the BIA in Alaska and Oklahoma.[122]

They appeal to Superintendent of the Papago Indian Agency and failed.[123] Further appeal to Phoenix Area Director of BIA hearing but again failed.[124] The sole reason for denial was because Ruizes resided outside the boundaries of the Papago Reservation.[125] The respondent -> Secretary -> claiming. as a matter of statutory interpretation, entitlement to the general assistance for which they had applied.[126]

The Court of appeal's reversed District Court's summary judgment for the Secretary[127] because the

---

[121] *See* Id.
[122] *See* Id.
[123] *See* Id.
[124] *See* Id.
[125] *See* Id.
[126] *See* Id.
[127] *See* Id.

manual's residency limitation was inconsistent with the broad language of the Synder Act, 25 U.S.C. §13, "that Congress intended general assistance benefits to be available to all Indians, including those in the position of the Ruizes".[128]

Thus subsequent actions of Congress in appropriating funds for the BIA general assistance program did not serve to ratify the imposed limitation.[129] The dissent took the position the Secretary's policy was within the broad discretionary authority delegated to the Secretary by Congress with respect to the allocation of limited funds.[130]

Language of the Snyder Act (or) Appropriations Act impose any geographical limitation on the availability of general assistance benefits and does not prescribe eligibility requirements or the details of any program.[131]

---

[128] *See* Id.
[129] *See* Id.
[130] *See* Id.

The general assistance program is designed by the BIA to provide direct financial aide to needy Indians where other channels of relief, federal, state, and tribal, are not available.[132]

Formal budget request submitted by Congress by the BIA for fiscal 1968, the program describe as follows:[133] "General assistance will be provided to needy Indians who are not eligible for public assistance under the Social security Act …and for whom such assistance is not available from established welfare agencies or through tribal resources…".[134]

whether geographical limitation placed on general assistance eligibility by BIA are consistent with congressional intent (and) meaning of applicable statutes

---

[131] *See* Id.
[132] *See* Id.
[133] *See* Id.
[134] *See* Id.

(or), that is, whether the congressional appropriations are properly limited by the BIA's restrictions.[135]

The secretary states the Act is merely an enabling act is merely an enabling act with no definition of the scope of the general assistance program... (and) Congress did not intend to expand the program beyond that presented to it by the BIA request.[136] There, she points to the "on reservations" limitation in the Manual and suggest that Congress was well acquainted with that limitation, and that, by legislation in the light of the Manual's limitation provision, its appropriation amounted to a ratification of the BIA's definitive practice.[137]

In recent years, Congress twice rejected proposals that clearly would have provided off-reservation general assistance for Indians.[138] Thus, Congress has appropriated

---

[135] *See* Id.
[136] *See* Id.
[137] *See* Id.

no funds for general assistance for off-reservation Indians, and as practical matter, the Secretary is unable to provide such a program[139]

Only need to ascertain the intent of Congress with respect to those Indian claimants in the case before use.[140] Some weight to budget requests consistently contained "on reservations" general assistance language (and) testimony before successive appropriations subcommittees to the effect that assistance of this kind as customarily so restricted.[141]

The Actual practice -> general assistance clearly has not been limited to reservation Indians.[142] There was testimony in several of the hearings that the BIA, in fact, was not limited[143] Additionally, the language "on

---

[138] *See* Id.
[139] *See* Id.
[140] *See* Id.
[141] *See* Id.
[142] *See* Id.
[143] *See* Id.

reservation" has never appeared on the final appropriation bills[144] The BIA itself made continual representations to the appropriations subcommittees that nonurban Indians living "near" a reservation were eligible for BIA services[145]

Although legislative history and formal budget request defined otherwise, the BIA no infrequently has indicated that living "on or near" a reservation equates with living "on" it.[146] Even though found congressional appropriation was intended to cover "on or near", does not mean Secretary is without power to create reasonable classifications and eligibility requirements in order to allocate the limited funds available to him for this purpose.[147]

Thus, if no enough funds for that particular area, the incumbent upon BIA to develop standard to deal with

---

[144] *See* Id.
[145] *See* Id.
[146] *See* Id.
[147] *See* Dandridge v. Williams, 397 U.S. 471 (1979; Jefferson v. Hackney, 406 U.S. 535 (1972)

problem -> then other lose benefits.[148]Agency must at minimum let the standard be generally known so as to assure that it being applied consistently and so as to avoid both the reality and the appearance of arbitrary denial of benefits to potential beneficiaries.[149] Assuming so, the question is whether this has been validly accomplished[150]

The power of an administrative agency to administer a congressional created an funded program necessarily required the formulation of policy and the making of rules to fill any gap left, implicitly or explicitly, by Congress.[151] Indian affairs -> agencies responsibilities -> *consistent and procedures that conform to law.*[152]

APA § 552(a)(1)(D) -> Publication required if substantial right [153] BIA chose not to publish its eligibility

---

[148] *See* Id.

[149] *See* Id.

[150] *See* Id.

[151] *See* Id.

[152] See *NLRB V. Wyman-Gordon Co., 394 U.S. 759, 764 (1969) (plurality opinion)*

requirements for general assistances.[154] Only other source of policy was BIA's Manual which by own admission was solely an internal-operations brochure intended to cover policies and "do not relate to the public."[155]

Rights of individuals = More rigorous than otherwise would be required (internal procedures).[156] Manual -> all directives that inform the public privileges and benefits available and of eligibility requirements must be published -> therefore must follow own rules.[157]

    a. Amicus: Whether memo constitutes general statement of policy

Therefore, the question turns on the availability of the information, how that information is furnished to the public, and if that policy or rulemaking.[158] General Policy

---

[153] *See* Id.
[154] *See* Id.
[155] *See* Id.
[156] (Service v. Dulles, 354 U.S. 363, 388 (1957); Vitarelli V. Seaton, 359 U.S. 535, 539-540 (1959)
[157] *See* Id.

Statements Are Pronouncements that Advise the Public[159]

Prospectively About the Way an Agency Will Exercise

Discretionary Authority.[160]

The Fifth Circuit Erred in Requiring Policy

Statements To Leave Lower- Level Agency Officials "Free

To Exercise Discretion".[161] The Fifth Circuit's Holding Is

at Odds with Constitutionally Grounded Hierarchical

Agency Structure as Reflected in the APA's Text. [162]Requi

ring Notice and Comment for Internally Binding Agency

Pronouncements Undermines Sound Agency Practice.[163]

Internally Binding Agency Guidance Serves the Public's

Interests in Predictable and Transparent Agency Action. [164]

---

[158] Derek T. Ho (Counsel of Record), Joanna T. Zhang, Tyeesha I. Dixonm Kellogg, Huber, Hansen, Todd, Evans & Fiegel (P.L.L.C.), No. 15-674, United States of America, Et Al., v. State of Texas, Et Al, Brief of Administrative Law as Amici Curiae in Support of Petition (March 8, 2016).
[159] *See* Id.
[160] *See* Id.
[161] *See* Id.
[162] *See* Id.
[163] *See* Id.

Policy Statements Are Not Subject to Notice and

Comment Simply Because They May Have a Substantial

Practical Impact on Third Parties [165]. A Substantial-Impact

Test Is Contrary to § 552(a)(2) and the Exemptions Carved

Out in § 553(b)(A) [166] The DAPA Memo's Potential

Impact on a Large Number of Individuals' Ability To

Request Work Authorization Does Not Trigger Notice-

and-Comment Obligations [167] The Fifth Circuit's

Approach Illegitimately Imposes Procedural Burdens on

Agencies Beyond Those Set Forth in the APA[168]

Guidance does not present Article III case or

controversy[169]. There is No federal-jurisdiction.[170] There is

a Violations separation of powers.[171] The Guidance is a

---

[164] *See* Id.
[165] *See* Id.
[166] *See* Id.
[167] *See* Id.
[168] *See* Id.
[169] *See* Id.
[170] *DaimlerChrysler Corp.* v. *Cuno*, 547 U.S. 332, 341 (2006)
[171] *Clapper v. Annesty Int'l USA, 133 S. Ct. 1138, 1146 (2013)*

substantively and procedurally sound exercise of

Secretary's broad statutory authority. [172]

The scope of authority -> unreviewable discretion to

accord *each alien it covers* a non-binding, temporary

reprieve from removal:[173] deferred action[174]; gives alien's

right lawful where Congress has made right remain

unlawful[175] and wrong, subject to removal at any time[176]

even though tolerate parents and children,[177] forbidden to

make work[178] wrong, INS contains no such senseless

restriction on authority[179].

b. Petitioners[180]:

---

[172] 8 U.S.C. 1101 *et seq.*

[173] *See* Id.

[174] *See* Id.

[175] *See* Id.

[176] *See* Id.

[177] *See* Id.

[178] *See* Id.

[179] *See* Id.

[180] Donald B. Verrilli, Jr. (Solicitor General- Counsel of Record, Department of justice), No. 15-674, United States of America, ET AL., v. State of Texas, ET AL., Reply Brief for the Petitioners, (march 8, 2016).

Respondents lack Article III standing: [181] None of respondents' theories satisfies Article III, [182] Self-generated costs,[183] Social services costs, [184] *Parens patriae*[185] , "Special solicitude", [186] and Respondents' theories would fundamentally transform Article III. [187]

Additionally, Respondents lack a cause of action.[188] The Guidance involves matters that are committed to agency discretion by law.[189] The Guidance is lawfull: [190]"L awful presence"[191], Social Security and tolling, and Work authorization. [192] The Secretary has discretion to authorize aliens to work. [193] The Secretary has discretion to authorize

---

[181] *See* Id.
[182] *See* Id.
[183] *See* Id.
[184] *See* Id.
[185] *See* Id.
[186] *See* Id.
[187] *See* Id.
[188] *See* Id.
[189] *See* Id.
[190] *See* Id.
[191] *See* Id.
[192] *See* Id.
[193] *See* Id.

the aliens covered by the Guidance to work. [194]The

Guidance is exempt from notice-and-comment

requirements. [195] The Take Care Clause provides no basis

for relief. [196]

Disability Claims, Guidance Documents, and the

Problem of Nonlegislative Rules[197]. Supreme Court on

Guidance Documents:[198] Fifth Circuit and the Prejudicial-

Error Approach[199]and the Ninth Circuit and the

Nonbinding Approach.[200] Different Reason to Hold Some

nonlegislative Rules Binding on Agencies. [201] Framework

for Considering Nonlegislative Rules,[202] where no

Procedural validity.[203]

---

[194] *See* Id.
[195] *See* Id.
[196] *See* Id.
[197] Frederick W. Watson, "Disability Claims, Guidance Documents, and the Problem of Nonlegislative Rules" University of Chicago Law Reviw,, p. 2039 (2013).
[198] *See* Id.
[199] *See* Id.
[200] *See* Id.
[201] *See* Id.
[202] *See* Id.

V. CONCLUSION

In conclusion, when turning square corners with the government, every actions leads to a step towards a casting effect where the Agency will be responsible for their reasoning and the in which the information unfolds with respect to their policymaking and/or rulemaking.

Therefore, when creating the quick reference guide for loan officers, I will take the following concept into consideration as a maxim of a sort- And, as everyday citizens, we can now turn square corners with the Government where we are now aware that we are apart of the process- a contribution, a democratic one at that.

---

[203] *See* Id.

www.ingramcontent.com/pod-product-compliance
Lightning Source LLC
Chambersburg PA
CBHW030737180526
45157CB00008BA/3210